Abigail Adams

YOUNG PATRIOT

Abigail Adams

YOUNG PATRIOT

By Francene Sabin and JoAnn Early Macken
Illustrated by Yoshi Miyake

SCHOLASTIC INC.
New York   Toronto   London   Auckland   Sydney
Mexico City   New Delhi   Hong Kong   Buenos Aires

ISBN-13: 978-0-439-88003-9
ISBN-10: 0-439-88003-3

12 11 10 9 8 7 6   9 10 11 12/0

Printed in the U.S.A.
First printing, March 2007

CONTENTS

CHAPTER 1:
A Minister's Family

Abigail Smith was born on November 11, 1744. In those days, people used a different calendar than we use today. The dates were the same except for one thing. With the old calendar, too many years had leap days. In our current calendar, an extra day is added only once every four years, giving the month of February an extra day. Leap days keep the calendar in line with the seasons. In 1752, people in England and the American colonies began using this new calendar. It corrected the leap year error. Eleven days were dropped from September that year! At that time, Abigail's birthday became November 22.

Abigail grew up in Weymouth, Massachusetts. Weymouth was a small seaport town ten miles south of Boston. People began to settle there in 1623. Most people who lived in the area were farmers, and most families had lived on the same land for many years. The Smiths lived in a tiny old house with a large new addition. From her family's home on a small hill, Abigail could see beyond the farm fields to the coast of the Atlantic Ocean.

Abigail's father, William Smith, was the minister of the North Parish of the Weymouth Congregational Church. He was a kind, gentle person who cared deeply about his congregation. He planted crops on the land around their home, and he also owned other farm land.

Abigail's mother, Elizabeth, was the model of an eighteenth-century minister's wife. She was a fine housekeeper, an intelligent woman, and a leader in the community. Mrs. Smith was a quiet woman who did many things well. She made sure the house was spotless, meals were tasty, and her husband and children were well taken care of. She cared for sick people in the parish. She brought food and firewood to those who needed them. She even found spinning and weaving work for poor women in need of support.

Mrs. Smith also taught her children to help others. "We should never wait to be requested to do a kind office, an act of love," she said. Abigail often visited the sick with her mother and helped her with the weaving projects. This work helped form Abigail's belief that women should care for the poor as well as their own families.

Abigail was a small, delicate girl with pale skin, dark hair, and dark eyes. She was the second of the four Smith children.

Mary, the oldest, was three years older than Abigail. Their brother William was one year younger than Abigail. Elizabeth, named for their mother and called Betsy, was five years younger than Abigail. The Smith children could not play with other children so they spent a lot of time with each other. They were never allowed to run freely through town. The minister had to be serious and dignified at all times. His family was expected to behave the same way.

CHAPTER 2:
A Life of Duty

As a minister's daughter, Abigail was expected to set an example. She had to sit still and pay close attention in church. Sunday services lasted from morning till night. The only break came in the middle of the day when everyone went home for dinner. All the children of Weymouth attended church and had to behave properly, but the Smith children had to be the best behaved of all.

When Abigail was ten, her father gave her a pet lamb. From then on, she looked after the family's sheep. She helped her father when the new lambs were born. Her mother thought Abigail did not belong in the barn, but Abigail did not give up easily. She usually got her way. A friend once told her, "You will either make a very bad or a very good woman."

Like most parents of the time, the Smiths expected their children to help with chores around the house. They believed that even young children should know the value of work. By the time Abigail was five or six, she could sew and embroider.

The heavier housework and gardening was done by servants. But there was no chore that Elizabeth Smith did not know how to do herself. "It is important for you to know everything about your household," Mrs. Smith told her daughters.

Mrs. Smith also taught her daughters to accept what life gave them. "We cannot know what life will demand of us," she said. "So we must be prepared to do whatever is necessary. If you are fortunate, you will have others to direct. But you still must know how to direct them."

In eighteenth-century New England, young women were expected to marry and raise families. Girls were taught to read English, write their names, do simple arithmetic, cook, sew, and keep house. They also learned how to raise chickens, grow a garden, make medicines from herbs, and take care of sick people. Some wealthy girls were taught to play musical instruments and display proper etiquette in front of company. They might study history and literature, or learn to speak French. They might also practice painting or dance.

Abigail learned everything that girls were expected to know. But she was never satisfied—there was always more to learn. No subject bored her. She read as much and as often as she could.

According to law, all towns in Massachusetts had to provide schools for boys. Girls were rarely taught Greek or Latin as boys were. Girls might attend classes in schools before or after the boys. Women sometimes taught classes for girls in their homes, but most girls learned what they could from their parents.

The Smith girls were lucky. Their parents taught all their children to read and write. Unlike most ministers of the time, William Smith was a college graduate. He had attended Harvard College. He kept a good library, and he passed his love of reading on to his daughters. He encouraged them to read whatever they liked. William Smith used the plays of Shakespeare, the poems of John Milton, and translations of Greek and Roman classics to educate his children. The girls also read books about history, theology, and politics.

Abigail quickly picked up her father's love of learning and wanted to go to school. Her mother worried about the health of Abigail and her other daughters. She feared they would be sick more often if they went to school. In fact, Abigail was often sick and spent much of her time indoors. Elizabeth Smith also did not think girls should go to school. She thought Abigail read too much for her own good.

CHAPTER 3:
Away from Home

When Abigail was a child, it was common for families to visit relatives' homes for weeks at a time. Travel was difficult, especially during the winter. People looked forward to having house guests for a month or two. They shared meals, games, and conversation. Guests brought variety and change to a house.

Abigail had no friends her own age in Weymouth. Because she was often lonely, she looked forward to spending time with her relatives. Sometimes she traveled

alone. Other times, she went with her
sisters.

Abigail loved visiting Grandmother
and Grandfather Quincy, her mother's

parents. They lived in Braintree,
Massachusetts, four miles from
Weymouth. Abigail traveled to their
estate, Mount Wollaston, by carriage.

The huge house on a hill had a beautiful view of the Atlantic Ocean. Abigail stayed at Mount Wollaston almost as often as she stayed at home. She sometimes went there to recover when she was ill. When she was well, she and Grandmother Quincy took long walks along the rocky shore. As they walked, they talked. Grandmother told Abigail stories about their ancestors.

Abigail had her own ideas about many things. She could be stubborn, and she did not always behave as a young lady was expected to. This upset Abigail's mother, but not her grandmother, who understood her. Abigail adored her grandmother, and Mrs. Quincy was delighted by the girl's quick, inventive mind. Abigail once heard Grandmother Quincy tell her mother, "Wild colts make the best horses." Grandmother Quincy gave Abigail faith in herself and encouraged her independent ways.

Abigail also loved being with her grandfather, John Quincy. She spent many happy hours with him in his library.

CHAPTER 4:
Good Company

Abigail always enjoyed meeting people. From childhood on, she learned the wisdom of being tactful. She made it a point never to repeat gossip. Her father told his daughters not to speak harshly of others, to focus on the good points of each person, and change the topic to "Things rather than Persons." So she talked about things of interest. Most of all, she was a good listener. After spending time in Abigail's company, people often praised her charming conversation.

Abigail's cousin, Cotton Tufts, often came to visit. He was a doctor in Weymouth. He first came to borrow books from William Smith's library. Then he married Mrs. Smith's sister Lucy. That made him Abigail's uncle as well as her cousin! She called him "Uncle Tufts." Although he was twelve years older than Abigail, he became a good friend.

Richard Cranch was another frequent guest. He was a Harvard graduate, a

farmer, and a judge. He also fixed watches.
He took Abigail's thirst for knowledge
seriously. Richard was in love with
Abigail's older sister, Mary, but he was
shy, so he asked his friend John Adams
to go with him to William Smith's home.
John, who wasn't shy at all, enjoyed
talking about many subjects. So did
Abigail. They often discussed books
and the news of the day. Even Betsy
joined in the lively conversations.

When Abigail first met John in 1759,
she was only fifteen years old. John was
twenty-four. He had already graduated

from college at Harvard, taught school, and studied law. He called Mary and Abigail "wits," but he found them "lacking in tenderness." The girls thought John talked too much!

CHAPTER 5:
Bustling Boston

In her teens, Abigail paid long visits to the home of her aunt and uncle, Elizabeth and Isaac Smith. They lived in Boston, the largest town in New England. Mr. Smith was a successful merchant. Mrs. Smith was a clever, well-informed woman. With her aunt and uncle, Abigail found more freedom than her parents had ever given her. Her cousin Isaac lent her books. Together, they discussed their thoughts and ideas.

Conversations in the Boston house were lively. The family and their friends

talked about everything imaginable:
politics, philosophy, science, trade, and
literature, among other subjects. Abigail
listened closely and remembered much of
what she heard.

Boston was a bustling city filled with
people from all over the world. Abigail
heard many different languages there.

She tasted new foods. She enjoyed the
fast-paced excitement of the city—the
noises she heard, the variety of people,
and the mixtures of rich and poor, old
and new.

Abigail spent her evenings at concerts,
lectures, plays, and parties. The city
helped turn her into a charming,

knowledgeable young lady. Boston's finest gift to Abigail was friendship with people her own age, something she had always wanted.

Abigail was always close to her older sister, Mary. In Boston, Abigail became especially good friends with four other girls. Hannah Storer was her Aunt Elizabeth's younger sister. Polly Palmer,

another friend, introduced Abigail to
Eunice Paine and Mary Nicholson. The
girls explored the Boston Harbor, toured
Isaac Smith's warehouse, and shopped in
the city. They all remained dear friends
throughout their lives. They could not
always spend time together, but they kept
in touch by writing letters. In their letters,
they poured out their impressions and
thoughts. They also tried to expand their
minds and improve their writing. They
even adopted pen names from history and
mythology. In her letters, Abigail called
herself Diana after the Roman goddess of
the moon.

Abigail practiced her writing skills
and learned to express her thoughts. She
believed that happiness came through
knowledge and that education should
begin at an early age. As she wrote to

her cousin Isaac, "In youth the mind is like a tender twig which you may bend as you please, but in age like a sturdy oak and hard to move." With her letters, she did not feel so alone.

CHAPTER 6:
Friends and Partners

Two years after their first meeting, Abigail met John Adams again. This time, John found Abigail more grown up. Abigail's curiosity about everything made her an ideal companion for him. It also made her a brilliant, well-informed person.

By then, John owned a house and barn that had belonged to his father. He had ten acres of farmland and thirty acres of orchards, pastures, and woods. John's mother's house, where he had grown up, was next door.

John also had a growing law practice. To work, he often had to travel to courts in other cities. Abigail and John saw each other as often as possible. Before long, they found each other's company pleasing, and they fell in love.

Abigail's father thought John Adams had a bright future. Abigail's mother was not so sure about her daughter's choice. Abigail would not change her mind, so her mother did. Abigail and John became engaged to be married.

John's law practice and Abigail's family duties sometimes kept them apart. They wrote many love letters to each other. In one letter, John called her "Miss Adorable." He wrote that he dreamed of her and missed her very much. Abigail called him "Dearest Friend." She wrote that she longed for their wedding day and the beginning of their life together.

The wedding, planned for spring, had
to be postponed until fall. Smallpox was
spreading through Boston. The disease
could be serious or even fatal. Because
John traveled so much, he could easily
have become ill. He decided to try to

prevent coming down with a serious case of smallpox by getting inoculated against the disease. To do so, he was given a mild case of the illness. That treatment was intended to protect him from further sickness. John and his brother stayed at their uncle's house in Boston for about a month while John underwent the procedure. Abigail's brother William was inoculated at the same time.

Abigail wrote John a letter every day that he was gone. In one letter, she asked him for his opinions about her. He replied with a list of her faults! He asked her not to be upset, but to try to improve. He charged that she hung her head like a bulrush—a plant with drooping leaves and flowers—because she was always reading and writing. He also criticized the way she walked and the way she sat with her legs crossed. He didn't like the fact that she didn't sing, dance, or play cards. Finally, he said that he had searched for more faults for three weeks, but found no more. "All the rest is bright and luminous," he wrote.

Instead of being angry, Abigail replied that she didn't sing because her voice was as "harsh as the screech of a peacock." She said she would try not to cross her legs, but she also told him, "A gentleman has no business to concern himself about the legs of a lady." She made no other promises to change her behavior.

John returned home in May to work on his land. He pruned fruit trees in the orchard. He plowed the fields, built fences, and planted corn and potatoes. In September, he left for a court session in Plymouth. At the end of the month, he wrote to Abigail, "Oh, my dear girl, I thank heaven that another fortnight

will restore you to me—after so long
a separation. My soul and body have
both been thrown into disorder by
your absence. . . . You who have always
softened and warmed my heart shall
restore my benevolence as well as my
health and tranquility of mind."

Abigail had also been busy. She
sewed linens and shopped in Boston for
furniture for their new home. By early
October, she was sick. Her doctor told
her to rest. John sent a cart to Boston to

bring all her purchases home. He tried to hire servants, but he could not find any who were suitable. His mother lent them one of hers for a few months.

Finally, on Thursday, October 25, 1764, Abigail and John were married in Weymouth. She was nineteen years old, and he was twenty-nine. Abigail's father performed the ceremony. Afterwards, Abigail and John rode home to Braintree.

CHAPTER 7:
Peace and Harmony

John and Abigail Adams moved
into John's house. It had four rooms
downstairs: a parlor, a large kitchen,
a small room for a servant, and a large
front room. Abigail's family gave the
couple a grandfather clock as a wedding
present. When Abigail arranged their new
furniture, she made sure that it was placed
in the parlor. John turned the front room
into a law office by changing a window
into a door. A narrow stairway curved
around the chimney. Upstairs were two

bedrooms and two smaller rooms. The third floor was an attic.

They spent their first few months as husband and wife quietly at home. Abigail baked and sewed. John dug up rocks in the fields and fixed the fences. Abigail cared for the peach, pear, and plum trees. She tended the cows, sheep, and chickens. Their fruit, vegetables, poultry, and milk all came from their own land. The woods provided fuel for their fires. Abigail bought fish, meat, flour, sugar, tea, and spices in Boston. She also made most of their clothes. Soon she was sewing tiny baby clothes.

John and Abigail took long walks together. They climbed to the top of nearby Penn's Hill and looked out over the land and sea. In the evenings, they read books and newspapers and talked over the news. John met with a group of

lawyers every week to study and debate the law. Abigail visited her parents and grandparents almost every week. She saw her sister Mary often, too.

Only three months after their wedding, John left to attend a court session in Boston. While he was away, Abigail had to manage without him. Travel was difficult when snow blocked the roads in winter. Abigail could not visit her family. She was close to John's mother, who lived nearby, but she still missed John. They stayed in touch by writing letters. It was a habit that would last a lifetime.

CHAPTER 8:
Raising a Family

That summer, just nine months after Abigail and John were married, their daughter Abigail was born. Everyone called her Nabby. John was still in Boston, but Abigail's mother and sisters came to help out.

That year, England announced a new tax called the Stamp Act. John and many others argued that it was illegal. Violent protests took place in Boston. Judges refused to take part in the plan, so the Massachusetts courts were closed. John could not work, so he came home.

He studied and wrote articles for the newspaper. He became more involved in politics. After a few months, the law was repealed, and John went back to work.

In 1767, just before Nabby turned two, John and Abigail's first son was born. He was named John Quincy after Abigail's grandfather. John spent more and more time away from home. As his practice grew, he bought more land. They also hired more help, but Abigail still had more work to do.

John felt a duty to serve his country. America was fighting for its independence from England. John's role in the struggle kept him apart from his family for months at a time. Once, he gave up politics, but not for long. Several times, the whole family moved to Boston to be

with him, but they always returned to the Braintree farm.

John relied on Abigail to manage the children, the house, and the land. When he wrote to her, he gave her advice. "Make your children hardy, active, and industrious," he said. He also wrote that he was afraid the neighbors would think she did a better job of running the farm than he did!

When Abigail wrote back, she
described the problems she had in raising
the children and running the farm alone.
She told him about conditions in New
England. She said how much she missed
him. "Alas!" she once wrote. "How many
snow banks divide thee and me and my
warmest wishes to see thee will not melt
one of them." She found she was able
to write things she could not tell him
in person. "My pen is freer than my
tongue," she said. In one letter, Abigail

asked John to "Remember the Ladies."
She wanted women to have some of the
same rights that men had.

Their daughter Susanna, born in 1768,
was named after John's mother. The tiny,
weak baby lived only a little longer than a
year. For once, Abigail could not write.

In 1770, their son Charles was born.
Another son, Thomas, was born in
1772. John's political career took him to
Philadelphia as a delegate to the Second
Continental Congress in 1775. The
country was in turmoil. At times, John
feared for his family's safety.

In 1777, a daughter, Elizabeth, was
stillborn. Abigail was overcome with
sadness. Although he also grieved,
John felt he had a duty to continue
working to keep America on the road
to independence.

CHAPTER 9:
Travels and Homecomings

In 1778, John went to France, taking John Quincy with him. They did not return for more than a year. A few months later, he sailed for France again. This time, both John Quincy and Charles went along. From France, John and the boys traveled to the Netherlands. Charles came home alone while John became the first American ambassador to that country. When Abigail joined John in Europe, she saw her husband and son for the first time in more than five years. She didn't see Charles and

Thomas again until almost four years later. For John, it was even longer.

In 1789, George Washington became the country's first president. John was elected Vice President, and the family moved to New York. The next year, Philadelphia became the capital of the country. Abigail moved there with John. Social events filled her calendar, and she complained that she had no time of her own. Abigail missed her home, and she decided to return to Massachusetts.

John was elected to a second term as Vice President, but he lived in Philadelphia alone. Then he was elected President. Once again, Abigail packed up and moved. In 1800, she and John became the first couple to live in the White House. It was not yet finished, and it was cold and damp. Abigail hung clothes to dry in the East Room.

When John lost the next election, they retired. John wanted to be a farmer again. Abigail continued to care for grandchildren, other young relatives, and a steady stream of visitors.

In all her life, Abigail Adams never attended school, but she was still one of the best-read women of her time. Even so, she had regrets about her education. Abigail was a poor speller, and her handwriting was far from perfect. She never learned to read Greek or Latin. Because she felt these shortcomings, she always pushed for better education for girls and women.

Throughout her life, she kept up her habit of writing. She wrote a steady stream of letters to her children, grandchildren, and friends. She reported on her life in London, Paris, Washington, Philadelphia, and everywhere she and John traveled. She also wrote to friends about the books she read and of her fears and hopes for John and the new nation fighting for its future. These letters tell us a great deal about the life and times of

America in the early years of its history.

Abigail Adams lived a full life. She died at the age of seventy-three, on October 28, 1818. She and John had been married for fifty-four happy years. America mourned her passing. Her strength, honesty, intelligence, independence, and nobility of mind placed Abigail Adams among the great Americans of her time. Abigail and John's oldest son, John Quincy, became the nation's sixth president. His mother would have been proud.

Index

Look for these other exciting
EASY BIOGRAPHIES: